AWAITING DAY SEVEN

AWAITING DAY SEVEN

❖ *The Science of God as the Universe* ❖

MICHAEL G. SHEAHAN, M.D.

TATE PUBLISHING *& Enterprises*

Awaiting Day Seven
Copyright © 2008 by Michael G. Sheahan, M.D.. All rights reserved.

This title is also available as a Tate Out Loud product. Visit www.tatepublishing.com for more information.

No part of this publication may be reproduced, stored in a retrieval system or transmitted in any way by any means, electronic, mechanical, photocopy, recording or otherwise without the prior permission of the author except as provided by USA copyright law.

The opinions expressed by the author are not necessarily those of Tate Publishing, LLC.

Published by Tate Publishing & Enterprises, LLC
127 E. Trade Center Terrace | Mustang, Oklahoma 73064 USA
1.888.361.9473 | www.tatepublishing.com

Tate Publishing is committed to excellence in the publishing industry. The company reflects the philosophy established by the founders, based on Psalm 68:11,
"The Lord gave the word and great was the company of those who published it."

Book design copyright © 2008 by Tate Publishing, LLC. All rights reserved.
Cover design by Janae J. Glass
Interior design by Leah LeFlore

Published in the United States of America

ISBN: 978-1-60462-989-7
1. Religion: Spirituality
08.5.06

DEDICATION

To my children, Corrie and Chris—if we all shared your concerns and life styles there would be far more love in the world and our environment would be far less endangered. Chris was the fire in which I forged many of my ideas. To my wife, Patty, who tolerated my seemingly endless, spiritual, literary quest. At times it must have seemed that I was back in school, this time in seminary.

Acknowledgement

Thanks to Peter Sehlinger, author and Professor Emeritus of History, Indiana University-Purdue University Indianapolis, for proof reading my early manuscript for grammatical, punctuation and spelling errors.

Table of Contents

Foreword	*11*
In the Beginning	*15*
Non-random Evolution	*27*
Time is Relative	*45*
Believe It or Not	*53*
The Prophets of the East	*65*
Western Prophets	*73*
Universal Consciousness	*93*
Day Seven	*103*
Postscript	*111*
Index	*115*
Bibliography	*123*

FOREWORD

You may wonder what a doctor of medicine is doing writing about creation, the existence of God and our relationship to Him, and world religions. Where did we come from? Is there a relationship between creation and evolution? What does science say, and does science contradict biblical or other religious teachings? Must it be creation versus evolution, or is there really evolutionary creation? Is there a higher intelligence, Supreme Being, or Source in the universe? If there is, how is that Being related to us, our planet and the universe? What do scientists say, both believers in God and non-believers? What do the prophets tell us? Are the gods of all religions the same God? Well, as you will see, I have something to say about all of these questions. Notice I did not say answer the questions. It will be for you to decide if my thoughts bring answers, more questions, or are just out of the question as far as you're concerned.

I'm writing this because I have to. In one of those rare, quiet moments in my life, a thought arose in my mind, and I have not been able to put it aside. Rather it keeps growing like a great storm, clouds piling on others, building, spreading. That quiet moment may have actually come in church. I don't remember. Not with a greatly moving or religious service that I can remember, but just one of those times when I was able to put aside my cares and reflect on things other than my family, home, and practice. Or it could have occurred while quietly sitting in my canoe, fishing rather than catching. I wish that I could tell you the heavens parted and a booming voice told me to write, but that didn't happen. In fact, as you will see later, I don't believe in booming voices, even for Abraham or Moses.

I intend this book for believers as well as nonbelievers. This is not intended to just be another book demonstrating that science and religion are compatible or can comfortably co-existent. There are many such books, and a number done well. I do intend to dispute those scientists who believe science either disproves the existence of or need for God and religious beliefs.

The thought was simple enough. We were not created by God, but of God, a piece of God. Suddenly, it was the only way that the science I practice could fit with the spirituality and faith that I have. Many things historical and scientific began to make more sense. To explain this concept I will be using a King James Bible version based on the 1611 translation.[1] But as we know translations vary, so the exactness of the translation, to me, is not important. The actual historical validity of the Word has often been questioned, as we will later discuss. Richard Dawkins in his best seller *The God Delusion* uncomprisingly questions the Bible's validity.[2] If you are Christian or Jew and believe in the literalness of the Bible, you will have difficulty with the first chapter, since I accept the Bible's concepts and story but question its literalness. However, if you keep a questioning and open mind, and consider the humanity of those who gave us the Bible, their attempt to record that which they did not see or experience, and record that which was first handed down by storyteller to teller, you may understand my premise. I refer to God as "He," deferring to tradition, but my God is genderless, or rather all genders. The translation of the Koran/Qurān used is *The Meaning of the Glorious*

Qurān, an explanatory translation by Mohammed Marmaduke Pickthall.[3] Much of the science comes from David Filkin's *Stephen Hawking's Universe, The Cosmos Explained.*[4] I must confess that I found this much easier to understand than Hawking's tenth anniversary edition of *A Brief History of Time*[5], although I do also reference his original work. My insight into eastern and mystical religions comes from Fritjof Capra's *The Tao of Physics,*[6] chosen for its breadth as well as its detail. Other references are cited in the text, with a full bibliography at the end, when you get there. But to get there we must begin. So, in the beginning...

In The Beginning

In the beginning, what? Science tells us that an entity of compact size, enormous mass and energy rapidly expanded in the "big bang." Where this entity of infinite density, referred to as a singularity, was, how it came into being, and into what it expanded is unclear. But expand it did, becoming the universe and our solar system as we know it. The very instant of the expansion or explosion seems to defy physical laws, at least those of Einstein's Theory of General Relativity. But an instant later the chaos of the creation and subsequent expansion of the universe obeyed the laws of physics. The time lines of creation are long, extremely long, measured in billions of years. This cosmological creation differs from biblical creation, not only in time spans but in the evolving order of the cosmos and the development of life on our planet. The biblical first six days have stretched for an estimated 13.7 billion years according to geological and astrophysical science, and are not over yet. To understand the biblical creation given these time lines, we will need to compare and match the biblical narrative of creation found in Genesis to the geological and cosmologic history of the universe and of earth as science knows it.

But, you ask, why bother? There are many books written about creation arguing for scenarios ranging from literal biblical interpretation, ignoring science, to pure science with evolution as the explanation for the earth's development and appearance of life. These latter explanations either totally discount the biblical story of creation in Genesis as a fable, or conclude that the Bible is non-historical but rather allegorical or purely symbolic, as the words that we write are symbolic of our thoughts. And, as we will see, there are authors who have worked very hard, stretching their religion and science to make the literal reading of the Bible completely compatible with science as we know it.

However, to develop my argument for what I call evolutionary creation, and to set the stage for my argument that there exists a Universal Consciousness, it is important to "get into the head" of the author or authors of Genesis. When

I attempt to do so, I do not envision a group of Hebrew herders, sitting about a desert campfire, passing around a jug of wine, saying lets make up a story of how the stars, the sun, the earth, and you and I came into being. And, let's not tell it straight as we think it happened, but let's do it allegorically. (I would not, however, protest if you told me that a bunch of Greeks lying on a beach, drinking wine, staring at the night sky developed our astrological signs.) No, as often as I try to imagine what came to the Genesis author(s), I am repeatedly left with the word inspiration. They were inspired by something, someone, to record, as best they could, the story of creation from what appeared and grew in their mind's consciousness. Let's see how close that story comes to what science tells us happened.

The biblical first and second day comprise the dark void into which the entity, the singularity, expanded, creating great light and energy. Those days also include the 200 million or so years that the expanding universe cooled enough for the stars and galaxies and the heavens to begin to form. It was also during this period when all the elements composing our universe, our earth, and even, later, ourselves formed from primordial hydrogen and helium.

Then there came day three. Somewhere between 4.5 and 2.5 billion years ago the earth formed from molten rock, cooled, and life-sustaining water appeared (around 3.8 billion years ago). The geological earth dated by rock analysis indicates that the earth's land formation is about 4.5 billion years old.[7] Bacteria (the first non-elemental "life" form) began appearing 3.5 billion years ago when water appeared, evolving into photosynthetic cyanobacteria. These photosynthetic bacteria raised oxygen to levels which supported the evolution of plant life. From 2.5 billion to 543 million years ago (Proterozoic Era) cellular plants and fungi evolved. With rising oxygen levels, many bacterial groups became extinct. This represents the biblical "And the evening and the morning were the third day" (Genesis 1:13).

Although the Bible says that the earth brought forth grass and tree yielding fruit, this did not happen during the 3.5 billion to 543 million years I call the biblical "day three." Gerald L. Schroeder, physicist and biblical scholar, in his book *The Science of God*[8], attempts to meld the Bible and science by pointing out that although full biblical plant growth had not yet occurred, the genetic precursors were in the DNA of single cell algae that were formed at that time, allowing for the subsequent evolution of the day three biblical flora. Thus, he justifies the seemingly scientific inaccuracy of the Bible by stretching the science of genetics to allow the literal biblical interpretation. In reality, we can not at this time compare the DNA of the algae of which he speaks to the subsequent trees that did develop. However, given the science of evolution, scientists can infer that he is correct and that all plant life developed from similar, primitive forms of life. Maybe just not on "day three."

At this point, I must digress a bit. If we are going to continue to compare the cosmological beginning of the universe with the biblical story of creation, we must address the author(s) of Genesis. While orthodox Jews believe that the first five books of the Old Testament are the words of God, dictated to Moses in Sinai, many researchers have disputed this. They cite evidence that the Books of Moses were written by many authors, probably after Moses' death, and were inspired writings, not verbatim dictation from God. Conservative and Reform Jews believe in various degrees of biblical continuous revelation, and accept the theories that Genesis, as well as the other four Books of Moses, were not verbatim from God. Therefore, the historical accuracy of Genesis becomes more questionable, since fallible men were trying to preserve traditions and stories that undoubtedly first were orally maintained, and at best, spiritually inspired. Later I hope to link that inspiration to the existence of a Universal Consciousness. However with the questionable authorship of Genesis understood, let's return to the unfolding universe and our planet.

Between 543 and 248 million years ago (the Paleozoic era), great numbers of diverse marine and land animals evolved to populate the oceans and continental land masses. This time period compares to the biblical "And the evening and the morning were the fifth day" (Genesis 1:23). The biblical sixth day, the last 248 million years, brought forth a complex evolving animal kingdom, and finally man. And so the expanding entity brought forth the entire universe, our solar system, and you and me. Yes, I know, I skipped the fourth day, when the sun and the moon were "created" or formed. But that event is out of place, both in the science of the Big Bang, and when interpreting the rest of Genesis. This is one of the reasons I can not believe the literal time line of the Bible story.

If you read the Bible literally, a day is a day, and God created all things in 144 of our hours. But this is to ignore that the biblical creation of that by which we measure our 24-hour day, the sun and the moon, did not occur until day four in Genesis. Once again Schroeder attempts to meld the biblical story with science by explaining the "pre-sun days" (days one through three in Genesis) in a different way. He translates the Bible by returning to the Hebrew derivations of the words evening and morning, those being chaos and order. He then explains the "concept" of the biblical translation "and the evening and the morning" mentioned after each "day" of creation in Genesis. He believes that this "the evening and the morning" referred not to sunup/sundown days but chaos rising to order occurring during that time period referred to as a "day." Yet he still refers to this time period of chaos becoming order as a "twenty-four-hour" day. He persists in a literal reading of the Bible, asserting that "within those (six twenty-four-hour) days are all the secrets and ages of the universe." He explains the 144 hours encompassing the 13 plus billion years (he uses 15 billion as the age of the universe) by invoking Einstein's theory of relativity, explaining how different speeds and different gravitational forces can speed or slow the passage of time for certain observers depending on the observer's position and speed of travel (the subject of the third chapter). He has compacted the 13 plus billion years of creation before the first of the humanoids to be called Adam (marking the beginning of the Hebrew Biblical calendar 5,768 years ago) into six twenty-four-hour days. He claims that they are non-earth-based time, but are determined by a cosmic non-earth-based clock.

The time after Adam, "Biblical time," he refers to as earth based and dependent on an earth-based clock (now at 5,768 years). His cosmic clock reports time as "seen" by the universe at the start of expansion. I will not reiterate his reasoning for the existence of and definition of a cosmic clock (which is a chapter in itself), but he calculates this to be a "million-million" times slower than our earth clock. Fortuitously, 15 billion years would then equal 6 earth days. However, long before the birth of this first man endowed with a soul called Adam, the earth was formed. After earth's formation should not the passage of time on earth be real earth time and not relative time as observed by some non-earth-based observer? He argues that time changes only after the 6th day to earth-based time, only after Adam. This is necessary for him to understand the Bible as written, rather than rewriting it, as he would claim I'm doing. Substitute "era" for "day" in the Bible (which would send a chill up Schroeder's spine), and move day four to day one and two when day and night are first mentioned, thereby evolving our sun and moon along with other celestial bodies, and creation as presented in Genesis becomes a reasonable summation of the development or our universe, earth and all life.

Why limit God's creation to our preconceived notions of our clock time? Is the exactness of time in Genesis that crucial? God is infinite, and time is His to determine. Likewise, why feature Him, as Genesis suggests, as some man that looks like us, molding whole animals from clay, and placing them on a ball he's placed in the universe? "And God said, Let us make man in our image, after our likeness…" (Genesis 1:26). "And the Lord God formed man of the dust of the ground, and breathed into his nostrils the breath of life; and man became a living soul" (Genesis 2:7). Yes, we are made from that which makes up our planet and the universe, but why not made slowly, evolving from the first primordial elements into that which we are to become? Notice—I did not say became. We are in God's likeness because we all are a piece of God.

Actually, I am amazed at how close whomever wrote or contributed to *The First Book of Moses, Called Genesis* came, in the absence of astronomy, geology, astrophysics, biology, and the other sciences, to accurately describe what is the mystery of creation. But, as we are told by the Bible, Moses was close to God, and if these were his perceptions of the beginnings of the universe then such revelation could only have come from a knowledge imparted by that closeness. And if not Moses, then whoever wrote Genesis' creation story must have been close to God to be so inspired, to encapsulate in two chapters the birth of the universe, the formation of earth, and the evolution of life. While there may or may not have been a booming heavenly voice, the author certainly heard, felt, or knew God, and became aware of God's communication of the story of creation. How else could what has been written be so prophetic? The author may not have written in terms of space and time as we now know them, not being fully imparted with God's infinite knowledge. But he/they wrote in human terms, with the limitation of a human's ability to understand the communication received, and then to write plainly enough to express that which must have been incomprehensible. That is why the validity of the narrative of creation in Genesis is important. It implies that the God in us, of which we are a part, can communicate to us the unknown.

If you begin to believe, as I do, that that which we call God is the original entity, the singularity, that expanded to become the universe, then we, as all things that exist, are a part of God, not made by God, but created *from* God. God is the universe, all matter, all energy, all living things. The purpose of this book is to convince you that this is so, discuss the support for this concept, and the implications for us.

Non-random Evolution

In the Genesis description of creation, events happened quite rapidly. Is there room in creation to allow for the slow evolution of our universe, planet, and self? I will not attempt to write in detail the defense of evolution, detail proof for the scientific aging of our planet, discuss in detail the debate about gradual versus instantaneous origination of the species, or debunk the "young-earth creationists" who believe our planet is only 10,000 years old. Rather I refer you to the extremely detailed writing of Kenneth R. Miller, *Finding Darwin's God*[9], in which he does all of the above admirably. I present only a brief summary.

Although many philosophers and scientists, a number presented in Miller's book, have questioned Charles Darwin's explanation of the origin and subsequent evolutionary development of the species, I believe that "main stream" science now accepts it as more than a theory but as a scientific fact. In support of this concept, Miller quotes from a 1998 National Academy of Sciences report:

> It is no longer possible to sustain scientifically the view that living things did not evolve from earlier forms or that the human species was not produced by the same evolutionary mechanisms that apply to the rest of the living world.

There remains conjecture as to whether the slow time frame of the Darwinian concept of random mutation, leading to variation in a species, followed by natural selection and preservation of the beneficial variation, is correctly represented by earth's fossil record. There are fossil records documenting periods of lengthy unchanging life forms with more abrupt changes (abrupt, but still measured in millions of years). This has led some scientists, including Schroeder in his *Science of God*, to speculate, by mathematical probability formulas, that there is some "direction" in evolution. An example he uses is the geological Cambrian period, when, after hundreds of millions of years of static life forms, there appears in the fossil record an explosion of new life forms. The relative rapidity of the appearance of these multiple new species would imply some intervention in what otherwise Darwin considered random mutation with variation. Those who believe in "intelligent design" use these periods to forward their theory that God intervenes and suddenly, from nowhere, creates a new life form and magically places it on earth.

This seemingly "punctuated" form of evolution has been explained by noting that there is evidence that within primitive life forms there existed the DNA information inherently needed to develop more rapidly a variety of life forms, just as our DNA continues to carry genes for more primitive animal organs.[10] Schroeder cites the occasional infant being born with fish gill slits as an example. The DNA information that may have been contained in the pre-Cambrian life forms lay latent until triggered by forces or catalysts not yet scientifically defined. What was the trigger? We do know that variations in the environment can cause differentiating alterations in organisms that in the same environment would develop similarly. So environment is a candidate for a trigger mechanism.

If periods such as the Cambrian explosion of life can be explained by the triggering of a preexisting library of genes, this obviously has implications on the "random" mutations leading to variation theory of Darwin. This would imply that there could have been pre-programming, at least an established gene pool, involved in evolution. This, to some, might imply divine intervention. However, this gene pool could also have evolved in a Darwinian fashion, just latent in expression. A preexisting gene pool does not necessarily imply determinism, meaning that the final development of all of life was predetermined from the moment that first life began. There is no need to reject the probability that "random" mutation with variation was involved in the development and expression of a stored genetic library. But what is random? Was the appearance of life a mere series of coin flips?

While Miller fully believes in and offers scientific documentation of the gradual evolution of all life forms, he emphasizes that Darwinian genetic modification occurs in a random, unpredictable fashion. He attributes the more rapid periods of species appearance to misinterpretation of the time lines and the amount of time needed to evolve characteristics of a new species. He emphasizes that "rapid" was a relative term, and involved millions of years. He offers scientific studies that suggest that there was plenty of time to evolve preexisting creatures into new species within these "punctuated" time periods without denying Darwinian evolution. Concerning the "punctuated evolution," upon which those that believe in "intelligent design" have seized, he quotes Darwin, who predicted such periods:

> But I must here remark that I do not suppose that the process ever goes on so regularly as is represented in the diagram (sic, a drawing of his from On The Origin of Species), though itself made somewhat irregular, nor that it goes on continuously; it is far more probable that each form remains for long periods unaltered, and then again undergoes modification.

However, I find no proof that the evolution as proposed by Darwin need be or was random. This would imply that, given the same beginnings, the same fiery to cooling earth, that evolution might have produced a world far different than that in which we presently live, and "humans" might appear and act far differently than we look or act, or not exist at all. To me and to science, random behavior is best exemplified by tossing a coin, which will turn up heads or tails 50% of the time if you perform enough tosses. True randomness is dependent on each event being totally independent and unconnected to all other events. The frequency of random events can be plotted on a curve that always becomes bell shaped if enough random events are observed. And yet Miller explains enough of quantum theory to be able to differentiate random behavior from indeterminate behavior.

Quantum mechanics state that if we know for certain the velocity of a particle, we cannot know with certainly the exact position of the particle, the second parameter being indeterminate. Heisenberg's uncertainty principle states that the more precisely we know the one parameter, the less accurate is our knowledge of the other. The example of quantum theory Miller gives is a beam of photons, packets of light energy, comprised of particles without mass but with wave form, passing through a mirror. While 95% of the photons will be reflected from the mirror, 5% will pass through. While we know the statistical number of photons passing through, we can not determine in advance, by the laws of quantum mechanics, which exact photons will pass or which will deflect. Yet the photons' chance of passing through is not random, since only 5%

pass. This differentiates indeterminate from random. If photons passed through randomly, we would not have the 95 to 5% ratio.

Although Darwin in his *On the Origin of Species* described random genetic mutation, I have found no evidence supporting mutation as being a random rather than indeterminate event. Miller himself blurs random "chance" occurrences with indeterminism when he discusses the lack of predictability of ongoing evolution.

> The explanatory power of evolution derives from its simplicity. Natural selection favors and preserves those variations that work best, and new variation is constantly generated by mutations, gene rearrangements, and even by exchanges of genetic information between organisms. This does not mean that the path of evolution is random in the sense that anything can happen as we jump from one generation to the next. Although the potential for change is always constrained by realities of physiology, the demands of the environment, and the current complexities of the genetic system, the input of variation into any genetic system is unpredictable. Although not completely random, chance does affect which muta-

tions, which mistakes appear in which individuals. As we saw earlier, this inherent unpredictability is not a matter of inadequate scientific knowledge. Rather, it is a reflection that the behavior of matter itself is indeterminate, and therefore unpredictable. It is one of the reasons why we cannot predict, with any detailed certainty, the future path of evolution.

To summarize, evolution is indeterminate, not random. Yet elsewhere he states:

God's means are beyond our ability to fathom, and just because events seem to have ordinary causes, or seem to be the result of chance, does not mean that they are not part of that divine plan. This is the reason why no religious person would take issue with a geneticist's assertion that the sorting of chromosomes in meiosis is random. Sure it is, every bit as random as the flipping of a coin, the impact of a meteor, or a sudden shift in climate that drives one species to extinction and allows another to survive.

Now, for Miller, genetic mutation is random, not indeterminate. Yes, flipping a coin qualifies for random events. Is a meteor impact random, indeterminate, predetermined, or determined by an active God in the Universe? Where is the scientific proof that sudden shifts in climate significant enough to drive life to extinction are random? Is that to say our present concerns about global warming and climate shift are out of our control? Doubtful.

While I believe in most of Miller's science, I don't necessarily believe, as he espouses, that an Eden-like place did not exist. To quote him:

> It is high time that we grew up and left the Garden. We are indeed Eden's children, yet it is time to place Genesis alongside the geocentric myth in the basket of stories that once, in a world of intellectual naiveté, made helpful sense.

The first humans connecting with God, that had souls, did reside somewhere. I'll call it Eden. Genesis, as I have already mentioned, is too accurate an account of the beginnings of the Universe, earth, and us not to admire the spiritual inspiration of its authors.

Miller also briefly addresses the origin of natural laws, the laws of physical forces that, with mathematical logic, govern our universe. These laws of physics involve, as he discusses, gravitational, electromagnetic, and nuclear attractive forces. The mathematics involved in calculating these various forces involve using specific numbers, called physical constants. An example is the speed of light. These constants have a specific value not predictable by any current theory. They just exist. With even the most infinitesimal changes in the basic physical constants governing the physics and chemistry of our universe, the universe and the elements and matter within would not exist. All of the authors referenced herein agree with that premise.

"Perfect" laws with precise physical constants derived from or occurred from what? Does a cooling accumulation of gases that formed the stars and the planets, including earth, bring forth from nowhere the mathematical logic required for such laws to exist? Or, considering that the laws needed to exist instantaneously with the "big bang," were those laws part of the entity before expansion? As we will see later, the laws governing general relativity did not exist within the singularity. Perhaps the expansion bringing forth our universe was one of many expansions, all failing by collapse or absence of matter formation. Then by evolutionary-type changes the entity brought forth the right combination of physical and chemical constants necessary for the development of our present universe. This would be survival of the fittest universe. But really more the survival of the only one that worked or we wouldn't be discussing it (the anthropic principle, thought by some to be an "easy out"). Yet, if the entity is God with all that it implies, why not get it right the first time? Or maybe there are multiple universes with different laws and constants, which, since they do not involve us, we do not observe. This is the so-called "multiverse" hypothesis.[11] These are unanswered, but perhaps not scientifically unanswerable, intriguing questions. An expanding source of the universe involving the indeterminate but not totally random evolution of life forms best fits our science to date.

Miller believes in God, argues that religion and science can co-exist, and even finds the laws of science justify the non-deist, free-will-permitting God who stays active in today's world. Yet Miller still speaks of God as separate from the Universe. It's as if he believes Saint Thomas Aquinas' view that God is required to be a nonmaterial, spiritual Being. In his book, *The G.O.D. Experiments*[12], Gary E. Schwartz also views God as a spiritual power outside of us rather than a part of us. To avoid confusing his spiritual power with the stereotypical picture of Michelangelo's God, which most of us envision, he refers to his G.O.D. as the "Guiding-Organizing-Designing process." His book presents a series of experiments designed to prove that G.O.D. is active in our everyday world, and that random behavior, sampling, or events are not the universal driving force. He uses simple experiments such as the repeated tossing of laundry into the air with his shirts never ending up properly folded. Seemingly his favorite experiment is mixing a sand painting and never recreating the original painting no matter how often he pours the sand. He uses these examples to note that the order we see in the universe is not randomly determined and that there is a G.O.D. process in the universe.

These experiments, however, are also demonstrations of the second law of thermodynamics, which is that isolated systems when left alone increase their entropy, or disorder. His shirts won't fold and the sand painting will not appear without intervention. To create order there must be intervention and the expenditure of energy. The question is, does that energy come from outside of him or from inside?

I would argue that a number of his experiences indicate that G.O.D. within him communicates with him. A good example is when he "asked" the "Universe," in other words thought or prayed, for another name for God and immediately received in his mind or imagination the name Sam. This peculiar response did not, at first, make sense. Later, he found that Sam, short for Samuel, was from the Hebrew Shemuel, which means "name of God." He asked for another name for God and received that for which he asked. Why must he believe that message came from without, rather from the God within? As if setting the stage for one of my upcoming chapters, Schwarz also discusses his firm belief that random events do not determine universal processes, and cannot explain the order seen in the universe.

I guess one of the greatest hurdles to accepting my theory that we and everything about us are an infinitesimal part of God is accepting that all the inanimate objects about us are a part of God. They were not apart from God. They were not sent by God for the use of the humans created "in his likeness." Could "in his likeness" mean not like a human photo likeness but actually an evolved part of God himself?

Certainly the asphalt or concrete on which we drive our vehicles, the vehicles themselves, and all the inanimate parts of which they are composed do not seem God-like. And yet they were invented by human intellect, designed by human artistic talent, and constructed by humans using earth elements fashioned by human ingenuity into steel, plastic, and rubber. They are part of the earth, part of the universe, and, like all of us, will return to those origins in time.

Despite there being perhaps hundreds of books written about the existence or non-existence of God, creation verses evolution, "intelligent design" verses Darwinian selection, theists verses atheists, and religion verses science, I have found no book with the premise that we and all around us are part of God. Although some would argue that I am just restating or reviving pantheism, which has been discussed for thousands of years, I disagree. While pantheism is the belief that nature or the universe is a God equivalent, the God of pantheism is an abstract God, not the God who became the universe, nor the God that is interactive in our lives. Classic pantheism does believe that since we are all part of the universe, and the universe is equivalent to God, we are part of God. However, in the most recent World

Pantheism Movement statement of belief, God is not even mentioned (http://www.pantheism.net/manifest.htm). Am I a panentheist? Possibly. Panentheists believe that all things are part of God, but that God is greater than all things. That belief actually allows that there may be other universes, other expansions, also part of the one Entity. Such belief also allows for a God active in the universe, even necessary for its continued evolution. However, as I will discuss later, panentheism does not support my belief that we all share a Universal Consciousness that is also part of God. Labels aside, I am not the only one with such beliefs. One of my former patients, Gerald F. Penca, drafted a paper in 2003 titled "Divinity of the Universe." In it he notes that "the universe has all of the attributes that we would expect of a Deity: indeterminate size and form, complete interrelationship, complexity and yet simplicity, with no specific origin and apparent eternal life." And later, "thus, it is reasonable to assume that the universe is God, and is therefore divine." He too uses the term God only out of convention "to identify the fundamental Being, only because of its general acceptance. Unfortunately, that term, as used by institutional religions, carries deeply entrenched connotations of negativism and separatism." Later, Brian Gallagher put out a plea on the internet in 2004 (www.aPath.org) to accept a new word for "The Divine Universe," combining words into "Diviniverse," believing "Divinity IS the Universe. The Universe IS Divine."

If God is creation, the universe, and you and I, the arguments as to slow Darwinian evolution versus punctuated evolution become moot. Evolution is real. It is God's way, either way. Whether evolution is Darwinian or punctuated, whether indeterminate or through the existence of an earlier DNA pool stored in prior species, is not really that important. That God represents order and logical creation is important. Magical, non-logical interventions, with God making appear on earth new species at whim, dispensing with or overriding the laws of nature, the "intelligent design" model, is not the God that I envision becoming the universe and all that is within.

If you can at all buy into the prolonged creation through evolution theory and that you and I and everything around us, as well as the entire universe, are part of God, you might still be willing to move on with me to investigate how others throughout history might have chanced on part of this theory. Being part of God may well explain the wisdom of the prophets. But first we must further discuss the problem with biblical time and address the arguments of the unbelievers.

Time is Relative

Einstein's theory of relativity was a boon for the writers attempting to understand how you and I, existing in the present, with a recorded history and an unknown future, with free will to change that future, have an entire lifetime, past, present, and future already known to God. Schroeder points out a number of the many examples of God revealing to biblical figures their future generations, the land in which they would eventually live, and the hardships that would befall them. Yet, we are assured that those same people had free will, and destiny was theirs to change. How is this explained?

You and I live in a linear time scale, with separation between past, present, and future, measured by our days, months, and years. These are dependent on the rotation around our earth's axis, and our elliptical earth's journey around the sun. God, the Universe, lives in relative, non-linear time. While I would not necessarily say, as does Schroeder, that "God is outside of time," I would agree that God is not bound by time. An oft used example of relative time is if I were to enter a space vehicle of the future that travels at the speed of light (oh should one ever exist!). I then roar off from earth and later return not one "earth day" older, yet hundreds or even thousands of earth years in the future, depending on the distance (number of light years) traveled. At the speed of light our linear time stops and past, present, and future are compressed into one. As Schroeder puts it:

> For the Creator, being outside of time, a flow of events has no meaning. There is no future in the sense of what will "eventually" happen. The future and the past are in the present. An Eternal Now pervades, like a cloud containing all times, not in a linear progression, but in simultaneity.

Although we have free will and can change our minds as many times as we wish, God still "knows," more likely experiences, our final choice and its consequences. Pierre Simon Laplace, the great French mathematician, held a mechanistic view of nature, believing all events have a definite determined cause and effect. He believed that if all parameters were known, events would have great predictability. While writing in support of his theory, he sums up the relativity of time and exposes his inkling as to the existence of a God as the universe.

> An intellect which at a given instant knew all the forces acting in nature, and the position of all things of which the world consists—supposing the said intellect were vast enough to subject these data to analysis—would embrace in the same formula the motions of the greatest bodies in the universe and those of the slightest atoms; nothing would be uncertain for it, and the future, like the past, would be present to its eyes.

Oh that he knew of which he wrote!

The belief that time is relative and non-linear and that the past, future, and present all exist in the present is similar to belief in the Akashic record.[13] The Akashic record, or better library, is thought by Hindu mystics to be one of the universe's primary principles. For believers, it is a record of all thoughts, words, events, and activities written in ethereal space. It is accessible to individuals in certain states of meditation or trance. It contains the past to or before creation, the present, and the future to the end of time. Some view the record as the cosmic or universal consciousness, a topic of a later chapter. The record is believed by some to be referenced in multiple biblical passages (Psalm 69:28, Psalm 139:16, Philippians 4:3, and Revelation 5:1). Nostradamus was thought to have had access to the record, as well as a number of psychics including the often inaccurate Edgar Cayce.[13] I see the ancient belief in the Akashic records as somewhat parallel to the biblical creation story, correct in the concept of relative, non-lineal time, but not literally accurate. Message received, not fully understood. As we will see in the chapter on consciousness, someone, or many some ones, seem to have been a part of the thought process that led to the concept of relative time long before Einstein.

As previously mentioned, Schroeder's belief that the first 15 billion years of creation and evolution were non-earth-based time, with biblical time, true earth-based time, beginning 5768 years ago, presents a problem to me. Once the earth is formed, with the sun, moon, and the rest of our solar system, then time on earth would be earth based, and that began 2.5 to 4.5 billion years ago. I reiterate this because his explanation for the life spans of the first ten generations of man documented in Genesis is also hard for me to accept. Yes, the writings have a historical bent, and clearly, the numbering of the families after the exodus from Egypt found in the forth book of the Bible, Numbers, has a very historical ring. Here the men age twenty and older, able to go to war, were all apparently counted, all 603,550. However, the first ten generations reported in the Bible lived 8304 years, averaging 830 years of age each, great health, but a Medicare nightmare. Schroeder surmises that there must have been some environmental change after the great flood, since biblical ages and sex maturity ages became shorter, unlike the generations prior to the flood (from Adam to Noah). Yet, if we are to believe the process of natural selection during evolution favors genetics that prolong the human race and encourage reproduction, his proposed evolutionary change does not make scientific sense to me.

I wonder if the generations with less historical impact were winnowed from the biblical record, as the history of the generations were passed down in story form? But, there I go again, non-literal reading of the Bible, and a number of readers are threatening to quit. I ask you to hold on, and then to tell me where Cain's wife came from, if only there were Adam and Eve, begetting only Cain and Able? (Genesis 4:17).

Continuing with Cain's family line, there seem to be a lot of women not accounted for in the biblical record. A prime example of generation compaction is found in Matthew 1, "The book of the generation of Jesus Christ, the son of David, the son of Abraham." Not a direct father-son relationship, but one having many great, great, great...grandsons before it, since there were a total of forty-two generations between Jesus and Abraham, and twenty-eight between Jesus and David, (forty-one generations if you read Luke, and, to be literal, also called by different names). Time in the universe is relative as are some of the time lines in the Bible.

If you believe in the literalness of the Bible, I am sure that, at this point, you are still able to rationalize the seeming incongruities found therein. If you believe, as does Richard Dawkins, professed atheist, scientist, and Professor of Public Understanding at Oxford, that the Bible is in great part inaccurate and of limited historical truth, you will still have a problem with my belief that the Bible is historical enough that it should receive at least a more epoch-type interpretation.

As an example, to demonstrate his disbelief in the New Testament's historical correctness, Dawkins quotes Robin Lane Fox, who "concludes that Luke's story is historically impossible, and internally incoherent"[14] including the familiar Christmas story. To bolster his disbelief, Dawkins also cites other authors who question the factualness of the Bible.[15] Frances Collins, geneticist and leader of the Human Genome Project, in his *The Language of God*[16] counters with "the more I read of biblical and non-biblical accounts of events in first-century Palestine, the more amazed I was at the historical evidence for the existence of Jesus Christ," and gives references to other authors defending the historical accurateness of the New Testament. (17–18). According to Collins: "the evidence for the authenticity of the four gospels turns out to be quite strong." I will not expand on the arguments pro or con, since proving the validity of the Bible is not the intent of this book. My intent is clearly to convince you that all that we know, both scientifically as well as theologically, is consistent with God being the Universe, and all that is within, including you and me. In contrast, in the hundreds of books written about Western religions, defending or denying the existence of God, the God in these books is always a spiritual figure, apart from all matter, or what Dawkins sarcastically calls a "sky god." This brings us to an appropriate time for discussing the believers and non-believers and their views.

Believe It or Not

In his ninth book, *The God Delusion*, Dawkins argues that God does not exist. He comes down hard against the God of the Old Testament.

> The God of the Old Testament (his caps not mine) is arguably the most unpleasant character in all fiction: jealous and proud of it; a petty, unjust, unforgiving control-freak; a vindictive, blood thirsty ethnic cleanser; a misogynistic, homophobic, racist, infanticidal, genocidal, filicidal, pestilential, megalomaniacal, sadomasochistic, capriciously malevolent bully.

After that, Richard, you surely hope that there is no God. He certainly might take offence. Dawkins also notes that formal religions have spawned many horrible deeds in the name of one or another faith, including the Inquisition, Crusades, and 9/11. The Old Testament certainly does outdo most, if not all books and stories, historical or fictional, when it comes to action, intrigue, blood and gore, wars with enemies both within and without, sex (heterosexual and homosexual relationships, consensual or non-consensual, adultery, and incest), and miracles bordering on science fiction, not to mention families in which brother kills brother or father, or vice versa. But was this all from God, or from fallible man, trying to interpret what their God asked of them? Francis S. Collins answers Dawkins argument that great harm has been done in the name of religion by stating:

> There is no denying this truth, though undeniably great acts of compassion have also been fueled by faith. But evil acts committed in the name of religion in no way impugn the truth of faith; they instead impugn the nature of human beings, those rusty containers into which the pure water of that truth has been placed.

I would argue that many wrongs attributed to religion have not been religiously based, but inflicted by groups of people with differing wants, economic and financial needs, educational status, and power bases. When engaged in conflict, these groups often are identified by their most identifiable, common trait. This is often their religion. However, they also have been identified by other common traits such as race. Certainly the Catholics and Protestants of Northern Ireland believe in the same God, read the same scriptures, pray to the same Jesus Christ, and have almost identical creeds. Yes, one answers to an Archbishop and the other to a Pope. But is this a "to kill for" difference? Is it not those in power versus those out of power, those connected versus the unconnected, and those more affluent versus the less affluent that promotes their grudge match, not their religions?

In Iraq's sectarian violence is it religious differences or political power that foments the discontent? The once governing Sunnis fight the Shiites that now possess the majority power. Are retributions due to religious differences or the former's misuse of political power? Is not their conflict in large part about who controls the resources (oil), and their outside political affiliations? Yes, the Shiites have their Ali, the son-in-law of Muhammad, and his lineage (Ahlul Bayt) that they chose for their leaders, and the

Sunni their Caliphs, beginning with Abū Bakr, as theirs. Yes, there are differences in their treatment of the Ashurah holiday and some interpretations of Islamic law, but it is hard to believe or understand that their religions, based on revering the same Prophet Muhammad and obeying the same Qurān, can account for the wanton killing of innocent Iraqi men, women, and children. Not only are the Sunni and Shiites brothers and sisters in Islam, but, as I will discuss later, also, according to the Qurān, the Jews and Christians who profess and believe in one God, the Scriptures, and who "do good works" are also brothers and sisters of Islam.

> Say (O Muslims): We believe in Allah and that which is revealed unto us and that which was revealed unto Abraham, and Ishmael, and Isaac, and Jacob, and the tribes, and that which Moses and Jesus received, and that which the Prophets received from their Lord. We make no distinction between any of them, and unto Him we have surrendered.
> (Sûrah II, verse 136)

It's not religion, it is land, wealth, and power that fuels conflict. Even Dawkins admits that the centuries' old problems in Northern Ireland are founded in much more than religion, but he claims that "without religion there would be no labels by which to decide whom to oppress and whom to avenge." I disagree. I'm sure we could find another convenient way to group and label them.

While there have been many atrocities committed in the name of religion, those represented and continue to represent the evils that can be committed by potentially good men and women. The Christian argument against God being all things has long been that if I am part of God and do evil, is God not evil? Only if you believe in predetermination. If my life has been predetermined and I can not alter my outcome by choice, then by some "Divine Plan," if I, being part of God, commit an evil deed then part of God *is* evil. However, if I have free will and choice, I can ignore my connection with God, and make bad choices. I can ignore my moral consciousness that connects me to you and to the Entity from which I came, give in to my base desires, and commit evil acts. God is not evil. The Hell that exists is my own creation.

Dawkins, in his chapter "The Roots of Religion," attempts to find reason for the existence and persistence of religion in the world. Finding it impossible to believe in the virgin birth of Christ, His raising the dead, and His own resurrection and ascension (although presented more sarcastically), Dawkins searches for some Darwinian natural selection process that favors the persistence of what he considers unscientific, unproven "irrational human beliefs." His conclusion is that religion is like a virus, passed on to our vulnerable, impressionistic children, and they to theirs. With his belief in natural selection he should not find it hard to believe that the monotheistic Israelite's God ordered Joshua to take by force the lands of other, polytheistic tribes, destroying men, women, and children as well as their animals and cities. Certainly this represents a fine example of the "survival of the fittest." And what drives some people that have no religion, no belief in God, to despicable acts? Is this not also an example of evolution and natural selection?

Interestingly, Dawkins concedes to the existence of an innate morality existing within humans, although he is quick to point out that we do not "ground our morality in holy books, no matter what we may fondly imagine." He presents an evolving morality from biblical time until now, citing the abolition of slavery, the rejection of inferior races theory, and the equalization of women's rights (albeit, unfortunately not fully evolved world wide).

This innate morality is not easily, or at all, explained by scientific fact, or even sociological scientific theory; not that many have not tried. It is not explained by Darwinian evolution. Natural selection would require such morality to confer increased survivability on an individual or tribe. It is this "Moral Law" that Frances Collins finds the most compelling reason for his change "from atheism to belief." In his chapter by the same title, he cites works from C.S. Lewis (who like Dawkins was an Oxford scholar) that brought to him the true realization that humans have a moral sense that is not shared throughout the remainder of the animal kingdom.[19] Collins speaks of the existence in humans of altruistic love, "the truly selfless giving of oneself to others with absolutely no secondary motives. Such altruistic love presents a major challenge for the evolutionist. It cannot be accounted for by the drive of individual selfish genes to perpetuate themselves. Quite the contrary: it may lead humans to make sacrifices that lead to great personal suffering, injury, or death, without any evidence of benefit." And Collins believes that "if we carefully examine that inner voice we sometimes call conscience, the motivation to practice this kind of love exists within all of us, despite our frequent efforts to ignore it." As we will see later, that "inner voice," that conscience, to me represents the God in all of us, in some of us loudly heard, in some totally ignored.

My belief that we and all that is about us are parts of God would be found too broad and flexible a belief by Dawkins, who quotes Steven Weinberg from his *Dreams of a Final Theory*[20]:

> Some people have views of God that are so broad and flexible that it is inevitable that they will find God wherever they look for him. One hears it said that "God is the ultimate" or God is our better nature' or "God is the universe." Of course, like any other word, the word "God" can be given any meaning we like. If you want to say that "God is energy," then you can find god in a lump of coal.

To all of that I say yes. Hold that wondrous lump of coal in your hand and marvel at the complexity of this source of energy, its density yet containment of great spaces between the electrons, neutrons, protons, atoms, and molecules of which it is composed. Yes that lump of coal had its origins in the Big Bang expansion of the universe, the same expansion that eventuated in you and me. I do not plan to worship that lump as a God, but am thankful that it has been provided for my warmth.

Dawkins fully expects that, given enough time, science will advance to the point that all of the universe, its beginnings and evolution, will be explainable. I am not sure this is true, but I hope that it is. I am sure that he and I will not live long enough to see it so. But I would very much like to be there if and when scientists are confident as to what occurred in that very first fraction of time when the Universe was born. Presently, in large part due to work by Stephen Hawking, in collaboration with Roger Penrose, "nowadays nearly everyone assumes that the universe started with a big bang singularity."[5] To be fair, Hawking is now attempting to convince scientists that there was no singularity at the beginning of the universe, and that time had no beginning. This is in part due to the requirement that a singularity expanding in the big bang necessitates a mathematical model of the universe in which the density and the curvature of space-time are infinite. Since mathematics can not handle infinite numbers, the theories of science break down, including general relativity. With the big bang singularity there would be a boundary for space-time, a beginning. Making this unnecessary, Hawking uses the quantum theory of gravity, "imaginary time," time calculated by using "imaginary numbers" (you may want to Google this one), and he advocates for space-time with no boundaries. "The boundary condition of the universe is that it has no boundary." "It would just BE."[5]

This sounds a bit like "one hand clapping" to me. Again, in fairness, what to non-scientists sounds all "imaginary," imaginary numbers do exist. They are as real as "ordinary" numbers, and, in mathematics, are actually necessary to calculate electromagnetic and quantum theory mathematics. However, this ignores that God, the entity or singularity, may have defined the "boundary conditions" and the constants, or the non-derivable fundamental numbers on which our understanding of the universe is based. As Hawking states: "One possible answer is to say that God chose the initial configuration of the universe for reasons that we cannot hope to understand."[5] Yet in his striving to develop a single universal mathematical theory that accounts for the universe, he is factoring out Supreme intervention. No big bang, no singularity expansion would negate my theory that God is that singularity, the universe, and all that is within. I hope with future scientific study we may, as Hawking himself ends both his editions of *A Brief History of Time,* reach a time when "we shall all, philosophers, scientists, and just ordinary people, be able to take part in the discussion of the question of why it is that we and the universe exist. If we find the answer to that, it would be the ultimate triumph of human reason—for then we would know the mind of God." But since I won't be there, I will go by proxy to the prophets, at least some of whom believe they already have seen God's face and know a part of God's mind.

The Prophets of the East

Judeo-Christian and Islamic tradition would require me to begin a discussion of the world's great prophets with Abraham. But to be inclusive, and that is what my God would be, I will start with the Greek philosopher Heraclitus (c.535–475 BC), Hinduism, Siddhartha Gautama - the Buddha, and Lao Tzu, founder of Taoism. Eastern mystic faiths or religions, in many ways, would accept my concept as all things are of God, with true "reality" being not that which we see, feel, hear, or smell, but which can only be sensed. In Fritjof Capra's *The Tao of Physics*[6], Capra notes that:

> Heraclitus believed in a world of perpetual change, of eternal Becoming. For him, all static Being was based on deception, and his universal principle was fire; a symbol for the continuous flow and change of all

things. Heraclitus taught that all changes in the world arise from the dynamic and cyclic interplay of opposites, and he saw any pair of opposites as a unity. This unity, which contains and transcends all opposing forces, he called Logos.

Heraclitus, therefore, demanded a dynamic changing of all things in the universe. Our universe continues to expand and change. Capra contrasts the philosophy of Heraclitus to that of Parmenides, who believed in a unique and invariable "Being." The reconciliation of these philosophies led to the Western philosophy of Descartes, of "I think, therefore I exist" fame, separating the body of humans from the mind of humans. To quote Capra again, this separation leads to a world familiar to us today, despite his writing this over thirty years ago.

> The mind has been separated from the body and given the futile task of controlling it, thus causing an apparent conflict between the conscious will and the involuntary instincts. Each individual has been split up further into a large number of separate compartments according to his or her activities, talents, feelings, beliefs,

etc., which are engaged in endless conflicts generating continuous metaphysical confusion and frustration. This inner fragmentation of man mirrors his view of the world "outside," which is as a multitude of separate objects and events. The natural environment is treated as if it consisted of separate parts to be exploited by different interest groups. The fragmented view is further extended to society, which is split into different nations, races, religious and political groups. The belief that all these fragments—in ourselves, in our environment and in our society—are really separate can be seen as the essential reason for the present series of social, ecological, and cultural crises. It has alienated us from nature and from our fellow human beings. It has brought a grossly unjust distribution of natural resources, creating economic and political disorder; an ever-rising wave of violence, both spontaneous and institutionalized, and an ugly, polluted environment in which life has often become physically and mentally unhealthy.

It is also a type of total separation that we do not find in the Eastern philosophy. To explain the difference between Western religions' belief in a God, external to our world, directing the world from without, and the Eastern image of the divine, Capra quotes the Brihad-aranyaka Upanishad (part of the Vedas, the holy writings of Hinduism):

> He who, dwelling in all things,
> Yet is other than all things,
> Whom all things do not know,
> Whose body all things are,
> Who controls all things from within–
> He is your Soul, the Inner Controller,
> The Immortal.

I would add your inner consciousness.

While Hindus worship many gods, these gods are found as characters in the tales, epics, and poems that form the basis of the teachings of Hinduism. Those tell us that all things and events around us are only manifestations of a more ultimate reality, Brahamn. In quoting the poem Bhagavad Gita, and Maitri Upanishad, Capra notes:

> Brahman, the ultimate reality, is understood as the 'soul,' or inner essence, of all things. It is infinite and beyond all concepts; it cannot be comprehended by the intel-

lect, nor can it be adequately described in words: 'Brahman, beginningless, supreme: beyond what is and beyond what is not.'- 'Incomprehensible is that supreme Soul, unlimited, unborn, not to be reasoned about, unthinkable.' Yet people want to talk about this reality and the Hindu sages with their characteristic penchant for myth have pictured Brahman as divine and talk about it in mythological language. The various aspects of the Divine have been given the names of the various gods worshiped by the Hindus, but the scriptures make it clear that all these gods are but reflections of the one ultimate reality…Brahman.

As we will discuss later, the Judeo-Christian and Islamic religions would have problems with this pantheon of gods worshiped. Muhammad, in the Qurān, specifically decries such supportive, surrogate gods. But that's jumping ahead. First let's discuss Buddhism and Taoism.

In Buddhism, you do not search for "God," but, through prolonged meditation, a mental process often requiring guidance and instruction, you seek an "unexcelled complete awakening." This is what Siddhartha Gautama experienced after leading a hermit's life in self exile, fasting and practicing deep meditation for over seven years. This awakening, achieving the state of nirvana, a form of extreme bliss, is not easily grasped or described, and not definable. But to understand what Siddhartha Gautama may have experienced during his deep meditation, I turn to John Snelling in his *The Buddhist Handbook, The Complete Guide to Buddhist Schools, Teaching, Practice, and History.*[21] In the experience:

> We might suggest that Siddhartha now finally saw through his "I" or ego, saw that in an ultimate sense it was an illusion, a creation of thought rather than anything with a more solid existence. Moreover, with "I" removed from the center of the arena, there was no identifiable subject perceiving the world in a dualistic (subject-object) manner. Consequently, "the world" became a unity. Siddhartha must also have become aware that the world of manifestation was an apparent outpouring of energy from a mysterious, unlimited source. During deep meditation, his mind perfectly still and quiet; he could feel the presence of this source, in totality, in his own heart-core. It was similarly in all other beings. Thus it was the true nature of all things, the basic ground of being itself. Never having been

born, however, it was not subject to suffering or death; thus it could be called the deathless. It was also fully conscious; it was "the one who knows"–though paradoxically it could not know itself.

Siddhartha became Buddha, "The Awakened One." Buddha felt, saw, and was one with my God. The Noble Eightfold Path of Buddhism: right understanding, right thought, right speech, right action, right livelihood, right effort, right mindfulness, and right concentration, each requiring separate but simultaneous wisdom, morality, and meditation, may be used to rightfully lead our lives, just as the Ten Commandments.

Not unlike the teachings of Heraclitus, Taoism, according to Capra, sees "all changes in nature as manifestations of the dynamic interplay between the polar opposites yin and yang." "One of the most important insights of the Taoists was the realization that transformation and change are essential features of nature."[6] Lao Tzu, considered the originator of Taoism, was a contemporary of Confucius. Tao, meaning "the way," refers to the way of nature and of the universe, constantly evolving, changing, with cyclical patterns. Like Hinduism's Brahman, Buddhism's Dharmakaya ("The Body of Being"), the Tao in

Taoism embraces the oneness of the universe, and, through meditation, you are able to sense and dissolve yourself into the ultimate oneness, the totality of all things. Excuse what may be a pun, but not a bad thought, to take time for you to lose your you.

Unlike the Eastern mystics, philosophers, sages, and prophets, the Western prophets named the oneness, the source of all things, God. They then proceeded to communicate with the source in a different manner.

Western Prophets

Before presenting the prophets of Judaism, Christianity, and Islam, I urge a word of caution. My belief that God is not a separate, outside figure or source of information and/or revelation, but that we are part of God, and "hear" God through our own insights as revealed through His spirit, will be hard to keep in focus during our discussion. The father figure in the sky image is ingrained in us. You may have difficulty not picturing a "sky god" with billowing voice, talking, or, better yet, yelling at our prophets. So when I use terms like speak and spoke, please remember that this is a voice picked up by no ear or microphone.

With that in mind, I begin with Abraham, the patriarch of the Judeo-Christian and Muslim religions. If you define prophet as "seer," or a person who speaks for God, he qualifies. He spoke up against his own father, heard God's will and promise, separated his immediate family from his kin, but most importantly he rejected multiple god worship and founded his beliefs in a monotheistic God. This is the mainstay of all three religions. Although Noah antedates Abraham, and the Prophet Muhammad referred to Noah as a prophet, Noah apparently heard God, obeyed God, but didn't travel about the country prophesying the coming flood.

The next major prophet was Moses. Not only did Moses hear God and speak to God, it is also written that he saw God, as did many of the Israelite leaders and elders at Mount Sinai. However, it is unclear what they saw, since God, at that time, appeared in fire and smoke in what to me sounds like a volcanic eruption (including the shaking). But God spoke directly to the people. It is difficult to believe that they were all attuned to God's "voice," since shortly after, when Moses re-ascended Mount Sinai, being apart from his people for only forty days, they turned their back on the God that lead them from bondage. A God that produced no less than multiple, sequential plagues, a pillar of fire, and the parting of the Red Sea. Hard to forget that! But they did. During those forty days Moses heard God give laws for the Israelites, including detailed construction plans for the tabernacle. I detail this part of the Old Testament only to make the point that we really do not know what Moses heard or thought he heard, or better yet, what he came to understand. But clearly Moses was well connected to God, had the best thoughts and wishes for his people (at least the faithful among his people), and wished to establish formal worship of God.

Following Moses there were many recorded prophets, men and women, including some whose writings became Old Testament books. Throughout the four Books of Kings, there appeared Ahijah, Jehu, Elijah, Elisha, Isaiah, Jeremiah, Ezekiel, and various others, including the recurrent unnamed "man of God." I do not mean to gloss over their lives, but for brevity, I will summarize their biblical appearances. The Kings of Israel and Judah seemed to call on the prophets to predict the outcome of a forthcoming battle or their own recovery when they were injured or fell ill. The outcome, in retrospect, seems predictable. If the king "did that which was right in the sight of the Lord" he won or survived. If he did "that which was evil in the sight of the Lord," he lost or died, and the people suffered with him. We never seem to learn.

While Moses was well connected to God,

Jesus of Nazareth was far better connected. As I believe, he was inseparably connected. Dismissing the Infancy Gospel of Thomas (which was dismissed by a council of ecclesiastics when the books of the New Testament were chosen), a Gospel which describes Jesus in his youth doing miracles and not very Christian like practical jokes, the first mention of Jesus in the Gospels was his appearance in the Temple at age twelve. It was then that He announced "that I must be about my Father's business." (Luke 2:49) I wonder how the child felt when He first began to realize His closeness to God. I wonder if it was swift, like lightning, early in childhood, or a slower process as He realized that He was so attuned to the God within Him that he could speak for God, not as a prophet, although He would prophesy, but as one not separable from God, as God Himself. My belief is that Jesus, who referred to Himself as the son of God, as well as the son of man, told us, that we were in a way like Him, human but part of God. He frequently referred to God as our father and to us as the sons and daughters of God, and proclaimed that God is "your Father in heaven." (Mathew 5:16) We just are not nearly as well attuned.

He further taught us to pray "Our Father

which art in heaven" (Luke 11:2). He did make clear that there was only one God, the one who had come within Him. "Why callest thou me good? There is none good but one, that is, God" (Mathew 20:17, Mark 10:18). "If God were your Father (which I interpret as meaning, if you realized that, like me, God is your Father), ye would love me: for I proceeded forth and came from God; neither came I of myself, but he sent me" (John 8:42). Jesus the man must have been constantly living Buddha's nirvana. Or perhaps, like Buddha, Jesus denied Himself that state of mind to minister to a suffering world and to teach others the way, as did Buddha. Jesus the prophet came to bring the word of God to the people. The spirit of God within the man allowed Him to speak God's words, as prophets had before Him. It was this spirit, or "Holy Ghost," with which the angel of God promised to fill the yet unborn John the Baptist. It was the spirit that also filled Jesus, the same spirit that John promised us, with which Jesus would baptize the world. "He shall baptize you with the Holy Ghost and with fire" (Luke 3:16).

Jesus clearly considered our soul, that nonmaterial part of us that the Hindu mystics call Atman, as the God within us, our Holy Spirit.

Our soul is our true self, not the "I" or ego which feeds through our senses at the feast of our desires. Some may reject the Gospel of Thomas in which Jesus was purported to have said:

> If those who lead you say "God's Kingdom's in Heaven," then birds will fly there first. If they say "It's in the sea," the fish will swim there first. For God's Kingdom dwells in your heart and all around you; when you know your Self you too shall be known! You'll be aware that you're the sons and daughters of our living Father.[22]

But in the same manner, Luke quotes Him:

> The kingdom of God cometh not with observation: Neither shall they say, Lo here! Or, lo there! For, behold, the kingdom of God is within you.
> Luke 17:20–21

Dawkins discusses one of the great religious mysteries, the trinity, and asks "do we have one God in three parts, or three Gods in one?" He quotes the Catholic Encyclopedia's difficult reasoning:

In the unity of the Godhead there are three Persons, the Father, the Son, and the Holy Spirit, these Three Persons being truly distinct one from another. Thus, in the words of the Athanasian Creed: 'the Father is God, the Son is God, and the Holy Spirit is God, and yet there are not three Gods but one God.

Dawkins also quotes Thomas Jefferson:

Ridicule is the only weapon which can be used against unintelligible propositions. Ideas must be distinct before reason can act upon them; and no man ever had a distinct idea of the trinity. It is the mere Abracadabra of the mountebanks calling themselves the priests of Jesus.

This dilemma bothered the Prophet Muhammad, for he was concerned that the Christian religion was headed toward, or already had become, a practice of idolatry or polytheism, similar to what was practiced by many Arab tribes. It was against this polytheism that he fought, and against which formed the basis of Islam. "Lo! Allah forgiveth not that a partner should be ascribed unto Him" (Sûrah IV:48). (This probably referred also to

Arab religions that worshiped sons and daughters of their idol gods.) "And the Jews say: Ezra is the son of Allah, and the Christians say: The Messiah is the son of Allah, That is their saying with their mouths. They imitate the saying of those who disbelieved of old. Allah (Himself) fighteth against them. How perverse are they!" (Sûrah IX:30). "They say: Allah hath taken (unto Him) a son-Glorified be He! He Hath no needs! His is all that is in the heavens and all that is in the earth" (Sûrah X:68).

Yet the trinity is easily explained if you believe that Jesus the man is part of God, made one with God, to speak with and for God, by recognizing within himself the "Holy Spirit" of God. "I and my Father are one" (John10:30). Muhammad, also a son of God, who also heard God (Allah) and spoke for God, has not to worry about Christians being idolaters. This belief in this Trinity will allow me to remain steadfast in the face of challenges even as great as the re-discovery of the purported burial vault of Jesus, and the claim that he married and had a son. He was not a spiritual apparition. He was a man, able to live, eat, sleep, suffer, bleed, and die. The difference between him and us is that he was also the perfect manifestation of the "Holy Spirit" of God, God within Him, and was God's gift to the human race.

God sent his "Word" in person to save us from our repetitive transgressions, committed despite His sending scores of prophets before Jesus. And like Jesus those prophets, for the most part, were ignored, killed, and/or forgotten. And, the "Word" still, for many, remains unintelligible. As was revealed to Muhammad:

> And verily We gave unto Moses the Scripture and We caused a train of messengers to follow after him, and We gave unto Jesus, son of Mary, clear proofs (of Allah's sovereignty), and We supported him with the holy Spirit. Is it ever so that, when there cometh unto you a messenger (from Allah) with that which ye yourselves desire not, ye grow arrogant, and some ye disbelieve and some ye slay?
> Sûrah II:87

Though Muhammad had difficulty with the virgin birth of Jesus and therefore His being God's "son," Muhammad did believe in Jesus the prophet, and his resurrection and ascension as was revealed to him.

> (And remember) when Allah said: O Jesus! Lo! I am gathering thee and causing thee to ascend unto Me, and am cleansing thee of those who disbelieve and am setting those who follow thee above those who disbelieve until the Day of Resurrection. Then unto Me ye will (all) return, and I shall judge between you as to that wherein ye used to differ.
> Sûrah III:55

Muhammad, the last great prophet (since no other has since come forth, as he predicted), was also close to God. He clearly defined himself as only a prophet, not a god, nor an angel. "Say (unto them O Muhammad): I am only a mortal like you. It is inspired in me that your God is One God, therefore take the straight path unto Him and seek forgiveness of Him" (Sûrah XLI:6). And to Muhammad, God's message, Muhammad's revelations, first passed by memory and by word of mouth, later written as the Qurān, was comparable to other scriptures. "He hath revealed unto thee (Muhammad) the Scripture with truth, confirming that which was (revealed) before it, even as He revealed the Torah and the Gospel." While Jesus preached social justice, like Moses, Muhammad received revelations concerning social justice, family relationships and especially the treatment of "orphans" and women. While far short of present Western standards for women's equality, his revelations that women should receive the "free gift of their marriage portions," (Sûrah IV:4) require four witnesses to prove their guilt "of lewdness," (Sûrah IV:15) prohibit "forcibly to inherit the women (of your deceased kinsmen)," (Sûrah IV:19) and preserve their belongings and inheritance if divorced (Sûrah IV:20) was progress in gender equality, although limited. This latter rule, if enforced in our country, would shorten many or our present American legal divorce wars. But "Men are in charge of women, because Allah hath made the one of them to excel the other, and because they spend of their property (for the support of women)" (Sûrah IV:34) is definitely not twenty-first century women's liberation. Also, the revelation that four witnesses were needed to determine guilt of lewdness was quite self-serving in absolving his favorite wife Āisha's alleged sexual compromise. But at least the Arab custom of burying unwanted female fetuses alive was prohibited.

Although the Quran provides some Islamic laws which to live by, the demands of Islamic faith are fewer. "And for those who believe and do good works, We shall make them enter Gardens underneath which rivers flow-to dwell therein for ever..." (Sûrah IV:57). "And those who believe and do good works: such are rightful owners of the Garden. They will abide therein" (Sûrah II:82). The "believe" is a request to believe the scriptures (Torah, Gospels, and Qurān), and believe in a single God, Allah, and ascribe no other gods. This is similar to that which Jesus commanded:

> Hear, O Israel; the Lord our God is one Lord: and thou shalt love the Lord thy God with all thy heart, and with all thy soul, and with all thy mind, and with all thy strength, this is the first commandment. And the second is like, namely, this. Thou shalt love thy neighbor as thyself.
> Mark 12:29–31

Both Jesus and the Qurān call for belief in one God and for us to do good works. The Muslim extension of this "believe" beyond a belief in one God, to a belief in following the laws and customs of Islam and Muhammad, derives mainly from the *Hadīs* ("Sayings" or "Traditions"), also called the *Sunnah* ("customs"), which we will discuss momentarily. It is this extension of "believe" that condemns Jews and Christians to damnation and the label infidel (anyone not following Muslim law and religious tradition).

While Muhammad led the nation of Islam to war, it was in defense of his monotheistic religion, battling against those tribes he considered idolaters, and defending his belief in the single God Allah. This is not unlike the Israelites, under the belief that they were abiding God's instruction, warring to claim their promised land, destroying the idol-worshiping polytheistic nations/tribes that occupied those lands. Was this God's "word," or what man believed was God's wish admixed with man's desire for wealth, property, and power? Did these wars represent evolution of religion, from polytheism to monotheism, decided by the survival of the fittest, irrespective of God?

I do not pretend to know God's will. It is indeterminable as to how close to God's will came this particular human inspiration to war. My belief is that these religious wars were fought by men given the freedom to choose their future within the restraints of natural law, inspired by what they believed was their obligation and their destiny. Yet Muhammad also espoused a God similar to the one I describe: "Unto Him belongeth whatsoever is in the heavens and whatsoever is in the earth, and whatsoever is between them, and whatsoever is beneath the sod," (Sûrah XX:6) but to me "belong" not as in ownership, but as a part of Him. The extension of the Islamic wars to Jihad, religious wars to spread Islam throughout the world, came as a result of Muhammad the man, as presented in the *Hadīs*. If continued Jihad is the will of God, and represents the "word" of God, then the loving God represented by Jesus, and exemplified in the Qurān, as well as the Bible, does not exist. Personally I believe that God not only exists, but that we are *all* part of God. Continued Jihad is not a battle for belief in one God, Allah, but a struggle to impose social laws and customs, derived by man, onto others.

For other infidels such as me, a better understanding of the Hadīs is found in the publication *Understanding the Hadīth, The Sacred Traditions of Islam* by Ram Swarup, an Indian and scholar of comparative religion.[23] Swarup explains that there are two sources of Islam, the Qurān and the Hadīs. "The Qurān contains the Prophet's 'revelations' (wahy); the *Hadīs,* all that he (sic Muhammad) did or said, or enjoined, forbade or did not forbid, approved or disapproved." Further:

Muslim theologians make no distinction between the Qurān and the Hadīs. To them both are works of revelation or inspiration. The quality and degree of the revelation in both works is the same; only the mode of expression is different. To them the Hadīs is the Qurān in action, revelation made concrete in the life of the Prophet. In the Qurān, Allah speaks through Muhammad; in the Sunnah, He acts through him. Thus Muhammad's life is a visible expression of Allah's utterances in the Qurān.[23]

This Islamic belief in Muhammad is a strong statement that his actions were God's actions. Yet, like all prophets, it is impossible to distinguish the inspiration that became his revelations as presented in the Qurān from the inspiration behind Muhammad's actions as remembered by others. The *Hadīs,* or *Sunnah,* provides detailed laws, rules, and moirés, of Islam. It provides instruction in nearly all daily activities, from bathing to toileting, cooking and eating, relationships with family and others (even animals), gifts, inheritances, dowries, sexual activities, and much more. These instructions or laws are all to be followed religiously, as Muslims attempt to imitate their Prophet. The adoration which Muslims bestowed upon Muhammad appears to reach a level of worship, as of a god, which Muhammad himself disclaimed.

The *Hadīs* are accounts and remembrances of what Muhammad did and said, traditions, passed on by word of mouth for generations, and eventually compiled in print. According to Ram Swarup, two hundred years after Muhammad's death more than 600,000 traditions were reviewed by traditionalist Muslim scholars. They attempted to vet and winnow all reported traditions to avoid spurious ones which had crept into Muslim religious life. The scholars attempted to assure the authenticity of the tradition or story, the originator of the story or Champion, and the chain of transmission. Various traditionalists accepted differing numbers of traditions, from 2000 to 7000. Multiple collections came into being, many dying of attrition, leaving six "authentic" *Sahīs* or collections. "Of these, the ones by Imām Bukhārī and Imān Muslim are at the top–'the two authentics,' they are called. There is still a good deal of the miraculous and the improbable in them, but they contain much that is factual and historical."[23] Remind you of our discussion on the authenticity of the Bible?

While some of the *Hadīs* appear to me to be

unadulterated, and have founding in the Qurān, the word of Allah given to Muhammad, many appear to have been less faithfully reported or remembered, and perhaps have had the meaning or import altered by the reporter or by the chain of remembrance of the tradition. For instance, in the Book of Faith (Kitāb al-Imān), when commenting on the faith of Christians on the Day of Resurrection, the tradition is that they will be asked: "What did you worship?" When they reply, "Jesus, the son of Allah," Allah will tell them, "You tell a lie; Allah did not take for Himself either a spouse or a son." (352) (According to Ram Swarup, the numbers refer to the sequential numbering of the traditions in the *Hadīs* collection, *Sahīh Muslim,* one of the "two authentics.") This will condemn Christians to hell. This I can hear and believe coming from Muhammad, as he did not understand the relationship between Allah and Jesus. However, after reading Sûrah IV, "Women" in the Qurān, it is difficult to understand Muhammad's sayings, as reported by Ram Swarup, "O womenfolk...I saw you in bulk amongst the dwellers of Hell." Further: "You curse too much and are ungrateful to your spouses. I have seen none (like them) lacking in common sense and failing in religion but robbing the wisdom of the wise."

I could go on comparing Qurān to *Hadīs;* however, it is not my intent to judge the various religions, or even the prophets, but to assert that we, the earth, the universe, and all the prophets, are part of God, and the prophets were close or "in touch" with God/Jehovah/Allah to varying degrees, and "heard His voice." I no more believe that Moses received exact blueprints for the tabernacle from God than I believe that Allah told Muhammad to perform ablution or purification by: "He washed his hands thrice. He then rinsed his mouth and cleaned his nose three times. He then washed his face three times, then washed his right arm up to the elbow three times, then washed his left arm like that, then wiped his head, then washed his right foot up to the ankle three times, then washed his left foot,…" (436). I do believe that Moses thought that the architectural requirements for the tabernacle would best suit worship and please God, as do I believe that Muhammad thought that his ritual of ablution was most perfect in Allah's eyes.

My problem with the *Hadīs* is what I see as the deviation from the Holy Book, the Qurān. Dependent on translation, Sûrah 48:29 translates to either "Muhammad is the messenger of Allah. And those with him are hard against the disbelievers and merciful among themselves," or "Muhammad is Allah's apostle. Those that follow him are ruthless to the unbelievers but merciful to one another." "With him" may be all those that believe, as he does, in a single God Allah, the scriptures (Torah, Gospels, and Qurān), but "follow him" may define non-believers to be any non-Muslim, no matter what their belief in the scriptures and their doing of good deeds. Despite this major difference, I find it hard to believe that Muslims sanction killing other Muslims, since the Qurān *and Hadīs* are clear that when Muslims meet, "The better of the two is one who is the first to give a greeting." (6210) "If you meet a Muslim on the road, you are to be courteous and step aside to give him the way." (5376) If you take your quiver of arrows into public, keep the "pointed heads so that these might not do any harm to a Muslim." (6332) Clearly, Muslims do not kill other, defenseless Muslims. What is happening in the Middle East?

The consensus of the prophets and mystics, either Western or Eastern, is that there is a single God or truth, way, or Body of Being. The Eastern philosophy is consistent with an internal source of that truth or being, rather than the Western, external God. If we are all part of God, with God within, should we not be able to "connect" better? Maybe not connect as well as the prophets or Buddha, but at least better than we seem to? Maybe if we take the time to be quiet and listen we too can hear the voice of God, a revelation, an awakening. But maybe there's more to it. Moses, Jesus, and Muhammad reportedly did not have to study, or spend years in contemplation to receive the Word. It was a gift, a gift from God. And yet, maybe the gift is available for the asking. "If ye then, being evil, know how to give good gifts unto your children: how much more shall your heavenly Father give the Holy Spirit to them that ask him?" (Luke 11:13). Again, "the kingdom of God is within you" (Luke 17:21).

Universal Consciousness

In his book *A Brief History of Time* Stephen Hawking discusses four major forces that permeate the universe, acting on all particles or matter.[5] The forces act as waves. Even when the force cannot be seen, the force can be measured by observing its effects. The force of gravity has no mass itself but consists of the exchange of so-called gravitons, particles without mass, between measurable particles or masses on which gravity acts. The effects on those particles having mass are what are measured. Gravity is a relatively weak force, but acts over great distance, and influences all existing matter. I say "relatively" weak force, but strong enough to keep the planets in our solar system dutifully orbiting the sun. Gravitational forces are always attracting. Electromagnetic forces are stronger, but act only on electrically charged particles. With positive and negatively charged particles the force may be either attracting or repulsing. The weak nuclear force is responsible for radioactivity, while the strong nuclear force holds together atoms. These forces, acting throughout the universe, act also on us.

We and all matter about us are constantly interacting with the universal forces. Therefore, in reality, no action is totally independent of all other things or actions. This lack of total independence is one reason Schwartz does not believe that order in the universe can be truly random. He points out, citing the forces in the universe, that the first condition of randomness can never be met. Repetitive events, such as even a simple coin toss, cannot be random because the events cannot be totally independent. Further, it is his opinion that "all material things—including living systems—are organized by fields, as well as generating them" and that "invisible fields play a fundamental role in all physical phenomena observed in nature and in the universe."[12] He describes a series of experiments involving both single persons and groups of people who, by "conscious intention," are able to "increase the organization of electrons flowing in a resistor shielded from both electrical and magnetic influence." This ability to influence was true despite distance from the resistor, even long distances. The degree of influence was proportional to the experimental subject's state of meditation, or absorbing mental state. The participants did not need to or were not asked to concentrate on the electrons. One group did not even know they were being monitored but were attending an educational session that included meditation and receptive learning. Using these experiments, what would be labeled paranormal psychology, as suggestive evidence, he questions whether our minds are not part of a "Universal Organizing Consciousness." Since the effected resistor was shielded from known electromagnetic and quantum forces, this implies that a mental force exists along with the gravity, electromagnetism, and nuclear forces. Like gravity, the force can not be seen, has no mass, but can be shown to exist by its measurable effects.

Schwartz takes the reader through a simple exercise in imagination. Beginning with envisioning a photon, having no mass, in the palm of your hand, he then asks you to sequentially envision an atom, chemical compound, cell, organ, organism, planet, galaxy, and finally the entire universe in your hand. Having demonstrated the power of the mind, he then questions whether there exists a "Universal Mind of the All" of which all our minds are part. Is this "Universal Mind" or "Consciousness" Schwartz's "Guiding, Organizing, Designing" (G.O.D.) process?

Such a universal consciousness, what I would term "God in us," others "self," soul, or Atman, might be an explanation for the questions that both Dawkins[2] and Collins[16] discuss. Dawkins ponders the almost ubiquitous existence of religions in society. Both discuss what Collins calls the "Moral Law" and Dawkins, borrowing from German, the "Zeitgeist (spirit of the times)." Conceding that religion appears in all societies, even isolated ones, Dawkins searches for a Darwinian explanation for its existence. Since he cannot find enough reason to believe that a direct Darwinian influence exists for the individual, one that would require religion to promote the selection and survival of that person, he explores Darwinian group survival or selection. Alas, he does not find this the answer. He does question whether religious belief might convey to an individual better health, but would view this as perhaps a "placebo that prolongs life by reducing stress." He also compares the love of God to the monogamous relationship between man and woman, when polygamy seems more natural to him, citing the human's ability to "love more than one child, parent, sibling, teacher, friend or pet." He finds spousal love to be "positively weird." He notes that the human brain is wired or chemically bent on assuring a couple's "love" lasts long enough to raise children—a Darwinian advantage. For anyone who has seen the motion picture *March of the Penguins* you will recognize this monogamous relationship in nature as being necessary for the survival of at least that species. He questions whether religions have exploited this tendency toward strong, monistic love to perpetuate their survival.

Dawkins finally settles on religion being a "by-product" of evolution. He notes that children believe and are taught to obey their elders, parents and other authoritative adults. This trait could imaginably convey survival benefit to the individual child, keeping them out of reach of the saber tooth tiger or the fire that would burn. "Natural selection builds child brains with a tendency to believe whatever their parents and tribal elders tell them." He also believes that we are all primed for religion by being "innate dualists and teleologists." As "dualists" we tend to believe in a separation of mind or spirit from the material body, at least in Western culture. Eastern cultures, as we have discussed, do not believe in that separation. Yet there exists eastern religions without dualism. As teleolgists, we believe that all things have a purpose. The Darwinian advantage to having these innate tendencies is less clear to him. He does offer that these mechanisms of thought might speed decision making and convey survival benefits. While Dawkins explores other ideas and references many psychologists and their work (Dawkins' extensive literature experience truly amazes me), "the general theory of religion as an accidental by-product–a misfiring of something useful–is the one I wish to advocate." His "gullible child" theory leads him to compare religion with the previously mentioned "virus" theory. He believes that religion is like a "virus" that children catch from their parents and authoritative elders, and then pass that "virus" on to their children. While this may be an interesting theory, it does not account for the present, real world experience. Presently, many organized religions see young people leaving their childhood faith, abandoning their churches, despite the pleadings of their parents (more often than not mute pleadings, since the parents have also abandoned the church). Yet, in their young adult lives, many re-seek some form of spiritual foundation, be it in our more recognized denominations or in other forms of social-contact-based faith. There appears to be something inside us that draws us to religion, the "god centre" in our brain of which Dawkins speaks, not yet found (a center, if found, whose existence would need Darwinian explanation to satisfy Dawkins).

While Dawkins concedes a moral "Zeitgeist" in us all, he is quick to point out that it exists just as strongly in atheists as in those with religious beliefs. It is the recognition of this innate morality, that which Collins terms the "Moral Law," which actually turned Collins from atheist to believer and eventually Christian. The most profound example of the existence of this innate morality is that of altruistic love or selflessness. This is giving yourself in part or whole, with no expectation of reciprocal benefit. Such altruistic behavior cannot be explained by Darwinian self-preservation theory, since often the behavior can be dangerous or life threatening. As Collins states:

> What we have here is very peculiar: the concept of right and wrong appears to be universal among all members of the human species (though its application may result in wildly different outcomes). It thus seems to be a phenomenon approaching

that of a law, like the law of gravitation or of special relativity. Yet in this instance, it is a law that, if we are honest with ourselves, is broken with astounding regularity.

Is not this "Moral Law" our Universal Consciousness? Finding the existence of the moral law within him, Collins questioned whether this represented "God looking back" at him. It also made him a theist rather than a deist, believing in a God who remains active in the universe. I believe that Collins' "Moral Law" is the God part of you, a God mind, existing within you, which nudges you to the moral high ground, to altruistic love and behavior. The fact that we all share this morality, share our God, gives us all a part of the same consciousness, making us part of a Universal Mind with a Universal Consciousness.

Dawkins, of course, seeks a Darwinian, evolutionary reason for the existence of this innate morality, that which he terms Zeitgeist. He finds natural selection and species preservation being benefited by parents being kind to and caring for their offspring. Although this comparison would account for the altruism of a non-swimmer parent jumping into the water to save their child, this does not account for the same behavior when a complete stranger is drowning. His second example of altruism being compatible with Darwinian evolution would characterize altruism as "You scratch my back and I'll scratch yours." This is not my definition of altruistic, which is having acted without expectation of reciprocation, Webster's "selflessness." Dawkins expends most of his literary effort arguing that the Zeitgeist exists without God, without religion (he would probably say "despite religion"). He notes experiments showing that atheists have title to this innate morality as much as, if not more than, those professing religion. He concludes from these studies that they are "compatible with the view, which I and many others hold, that we do not need God in order to be good–or evil." Unfortunately, he uses "religion" as being synonymous with "God." They are not. He should say, we don't need religion to be good. He also explores the many acts of man recorded in the Bible that might or should be termed evil. In doing so, he confuses the acts of man with the acts of God; albeit men often thought what they did was the will of God. It is God in Dawkins, a part of Dawkins, which lights *his* inner moral light.

Day Seven

For those who are hanging in until the finish, I thank you, and warn you that this final chapter has checked all scientific and mathematical proofs at the door. Let me entice you, as the song in *Willy Wonka* goes, to "look and you'll see into your imagination." That imagination is part of you, your inner self. Dawkins would dismiss all that follows as mere speculation, not founded in any scientific evidence. But to me it makes sense. If the first five days of creation took over 13 billion years, what makes us think that day 6 is complete? Are we not still evolving? Is the earth not still evolving? Is the universe not still expanding? "And on the seventh day God ended his work which he had made; and he rested on the seventh day from all his work which he had made" (Genesis 2:2). However, contemplating the world as we know it, I believe that God has not "ended his work." Preceding this biblical quotation is another, "And God saw that every thing that he had made, and behold, it was very good. And the evening and the morning were the sixth day" (Genesis 1:31). Now I don't know which of the multiple, never-ending, redundant "news" sources you use to obtain current information, but according to mine, all is *not* very good. It does not seem the time that God would rest.

And, in fact, he has not rested. The earth continues to evolve. This fact allows me to refute the concept that there cannot be a God because he would be cruel and vindictive given the natural disasters we encounter. The disastrous tsunami that struck Indonesia was not evidence of a vengeful God, but the slippage in a tectonic plate as the Earth groaned into its next form, continued evolutionary creation. I do not agree with the belief of some fundamentalist Christians that Katrina was the wrath of God punishing a modern Sodom. They forget that God would not destroy Sodom for the sake of even as few as ten righteous men. New Orleans certainly contained far more than ten. Furthermore, given the increase in crime following Katrina, both in New Orleans and in the refugee-abundant Houston, God certainly missed a number of the wicked if this was his punishment. Rather, the hurricane Katrina was the result of weather conditions both natural and probably man contributed, conditions that some day science should be able to fully analyze.

Wait, you say! Are not that tectonic plate and the winds of the hurricane part of God? Yes, God is all things. But God set the universe and our earth on an evolutionary course, following the laws of physics, to become only He knows what. Day seven has yet to arrive. To disrupt earth's evolution by divine intervention, circumventing the laws of physics, a true miracle, appears not to be His plan. Man continues to evolve. Over thousands of years our brains have enlarged, our knowledge has expanded, and we are more intelligent, although perhaps not always wiser. Man with free will and an ever-expanding geophysical science has just not yet evolved to be able or willing to address these natural occurrences in order to prevent, ameliorate, or predict them with enough certainty that we are able to respond. Presently responding often means getting out of the way. We have, however, with not always the best judgment, diverted waterways, eroded deltas, and destroyed wet lands acting as buffer zones to the sea, through our free will. We have called this economic development. We have the technical knowledge to create an early warning system for tsunamis. It is our free will to prioritize and construct such a life-saving system or not. If we believe in evolutionary creation, we must accept that the survival of the fittest demands adaptation to forces we cannot control, and scientific investigation of forces to which we presently are vulnerable or to which we have contributed, in order to develop appropriate responses.

It turns out that I am not alone in my belief of what I've called evolutionary creation. Francis Collins notes that this is generally referred to as "theistic evolution," quite possibly attempting to avoid any mix up with creationism. He notes that "theistic evolution is the dominant position of serious biologists who are also serious believers." He cites a number of prominent scientists, and also Pope John Paul II, quoting him: "New findings lead us toward the recognition of evolution as more than a hypothesis." But Collins also notes that John Paul II was quick to affirm the position of Pius XII: "If the origin of the human body comes through living matter which existed previously, the spiritual soul is created directly by God." I argue that the soul is part of God.

I do not have a firm belief concerning the

arrival of day seven. Will it be that day, perhaps millions of earth years in the future, when men have evolved a brain and spirit that ends warring and want? When we develop understanding and a spirit that protects our planet and all that lives upon it? How much further do we humans need to evolve to recognize our relationship with God? Will that recognition come as part of or after our recognition of a Universal Consciousness that we all share? Or will day seven be the day that the expansion of the universe ceases and enters either a slow contraction or reversal, or even a sudden collapse, imploding. Would that not give new meaning to "meet your maker?"

In any event, I, in my present form, will not witness the arrival. In the interim, what do we do? Hopefully we live rewarding and pleasurable lives, while all nudging the evolutionary ball forward, some to a greater extent than others. Hopefully, working together, we will not bring on the next great extinction. There were at least five great extinctions. The largest was approximately 250 million years ago when 95% of all life suffered a massive extinction. Massive volcanic activity is thought to have been the cause. The last was approximately 65 million years ago when an asteroid, over 10 kilometers in diameter, hit earth with such explosive force that it caused earthquakes, volcanic eruptions and a cloud of dust that shrouded the sun. The lack of sun cooled the earth, stopped photosynthesis, and subsequently killed the very large, cold-blooded mammals—over 50% of all animals. So went the non-adaptable dinosaurs.

These extinction events where out of man's control. But our next great threats are not. Global warming has the potential, through climate change and loss of agriculture, to winnow our population almost to the extent of the dinosaurs' extinction. Some will remain, and slowly adapt. But adaptation through evolution is a process measured in thousands, if not millions of years. Such adaptation is far too slow compared to the rapidity with which this disaster is progressing. And of course, there is always the possibility that a less-than-forward-thinking government will make small nuclear weapons available on the black market, as they have other deadly weapons. Yet the planet will probably persist, and God's creation will continue to evolve, and day seven will eventually come.

To avoid these and other human-made disasters requires us to be aware of our place on this planet, in the universe of God, and become more attuned and receptive to the God in us, to Collins' "Moral Law," Dawkins' "Moral Sense," Taoism's "Way," and Buddha's "Body of Being." We need to be quiet and listen for that internal voice or message, and share within our Universal Consciousness. We have within us this universal force with which we can affect the evolution of our world and of man. We need to explore it, learn to use it. Perhaps just living the Ten Commandments might be a start. Or for atheists that want their moral commandments void of God, we could live the "New Ten Commandments" that Dawkins found on the internet on an atheist website.[24]

> "Do not do to others what you would not want them to do to you."
> "In all things, strive to cause no harm." (This is one I know well as a physician.)
> "Treat your fellow human beings, your fellow living things, and the world in general with love, honesty, faithfulness and respect."
> "Do not overlook evil or shrink from administering justice, but always be ready to forgive wrongdoing freely admitted and honestly regretted."
> "Live life with a sense of joy and wonder."

"Always seek to be learning something new."

"Test all things; always check your ideas against the facts, and be ready to discard even a cherished belief if it does not conform to them."

"Never seek to censor or cut yourself off from dissent; always respect the right of others to disagree with you."

"Form independent opinions on the basis of you own reason and experience; do not allow yourself to be led blindly by others."

"Question everything."

I do not see in these any conflict with the religions that I have discussed herein. I hear in these, even without the mention of God, the "Moral Law" and "Moral Sense" that is the whisper of God within us. It's time to take time and listen.

POSTSCRIPT

I am sure that at this point, if you made it to the end, I have offended just about all of you in some way. Clearly the Fundamentalist Christian will label my liberal interpretation of the Bible and my questioning its inconsistencies as blasphemy. Christians in general will accuse me of misinterpreting the birth, life, death and resurrection of Jesus the Christ. Muslims will accuse me of vast oversimplification of their faith and culture, in essence ignoring the *Hadīs*. Some will question whether I equate Jesus Christ with Muhammad. I do not. I contrast Christ's "turn the other cheek" with Muhammad's apparent ease in beheading men, taking prisoner slaves and concubines, and bribing with spoils of war. However, this undertaking was not to provide such a comparison of prophets or religions, nor to rate them. Scientists will ask me for proof of my theory for evolutionary creation, for which I have none. I can only retort: Why did the laws of physics become applicable only after the instant that the universe began? Why or how were they, in the words of Collins, "despite massive improbabilities, the properties of the universe appear to have been precisely tuned for life?" And what scientific proof is there that my theory of evolutionary creation is incorrect? To answer all, it's simple. Given our present knowledge, it just makes sense.

I have found, during the research and writing of this manuscript, that I have followed a number of the above new commandments. I have definitely learned something new, attempted to test my ideas against known facts, and questioned just about everything. I definitely attempted to apply reason, although there will be many that find me unreasonable. I will now question all organized religions, since it has become clear to me that religious leaders are variously attuned to the God inside them. When listening to the extremes of all faiths it is hard to believe that we all speak for or of the same God. I guess the watch word is the biblical warning, "Beware of false prophets." (Matthew 7:15) If you believe in Jesus, either as God or only a great prophet, maybe the best advice would be to ask yourself what Jesus would do, what He would want you to do. He is an excellent person to emulate. One other piece of advice: take time to know who you are.

To again quote Collins: "Another striking feature of the human genome comes from the comparison of different members of our own species. At the DNA level, we are all 99.9 % identical." That similarity applies regardless of which two individuals from around the world you choose to compare. Thus, by DNA analysis, we humans are truly part of one family. So let's start acting as one, but not the dysfunctional one we now appear to be. And we would do well to, in the words of Dawkins, adding another commandment to those above: "Value the future on a timescale longer than your own." Day Seven is yet to come.

Index

Able	50
Ablution	90
Abraham	12, 50, 56, 65, 73-74
Abū Bakr	56
Adam	22-23, 49-50
Ahijah	75
Āisha	83
Akashic record	47-48
Algae	19
Ali	55
Allah	56, 79-87, 89-91
Altruism	100-101
Aquinas, St. Thomas	37
Ahlul Bayt	55
Anthropic principle	37
Ashurah	56
Astrophysics	24
Athanasian Creed	79
Atheism	59
Atman	77, 96

Baptize	77
Biblical time	22, 43, 48
Big bang	15, 20, 36, 61-63
Bhagavad Gita	68
Body of Being	71, 91, 109
Book of Faith	89
Brahman	68-69, 71
Buddha	65, 71, 77, 92, 109
Cain	50
Cambrian	28-29
Capra, Fritjof	14, 65-66, 68, 71
Catholic Encyclopedia	78
Catholic, Irish	55
Cayce, Edgar	48
Collins, Frances	51, 54. 59, 96, 99-100, 106, 109, 112-113
Continuous revelation	19
Cosmic clock	22
Cosmology	15-16, 19
Cosmos	14-15
Creation	11, 15-17, 19, 21-27, 42, 48, 70, 103-104, 106, 108, 111-112
Crusades	54
Customs	84, 86
Cyanobacteria	18
Darwin, Charles	29-31, 33
Dawkins, Richard	13, 50-54, 56-61, 78-79, 96-101, 103, 109, 113
Descartes	66

Dharmakaya	71
Diviniverse	42
DNA	18-19, 29, 42, 113
Dualist	70, 97
Earth clock	22
Eden	35
Einstein, Albert	15, 21, 48
Electromagnetic force	62, 93, 95
Elijah	75
Elisha	75
Entropy	38
Eternal now	46
Evolution	11, 16, 18-19, 24, 27-34, 36-37, 40-42, 48-49, 58-59, 61, 85, 97, 100-101, 104-109, 111-112
Evolutionary creation	104-106, 111-112
Expansion of the universe	15, 61, 107
Ezekiel	75
Filkin. David	14
Fossil record	28
Fox, Robert Lee	51
Free will	37, 45-46, 57, 105-106
Gallagher, Brian	42
Garden	35, 84
Gautama, Siddhartha	65, 69-70
Genesis	16-21, 23-25, 27, 35, 49-50, 103-104
Geology	24
G.O.D.	37-39
God mind	100

Gospels	51, 76, 84, 91
Gospel of Thomas	76, 78
Gravity	62, 93, 95
Hadīs	84, 86-91, 111
Hawking, Stephen	14, 61-63, 93
Heisenberg's uncertainty principle	32
Heraclitus	65-66, 71
Hindu mystics	47, 77
Hinduism	65, 68
Holy Book	90
Holy Ghost	77
Holy Spirit	77, 79-81, 92
Human genome project	51
Imān	88
Imām Bukhārī	88
Imaginary numbers	62
Imaginary time	62
Infidel	85
Inquisition	54
Inspiration	17, 20, 35, 87
Intelligent design	29, 31, 40, 42, 79, 84
Isaiah	75
Islam	56, 73, 79, 84-87
Jefferson, Thomas	79
Jehu	75
Jeremiah	75
Jesus Christ	50-51, 55-56, 76-82, 84, 86, 89, 92, 111-112
Jihad	86

John the Baptist	77
Joshua	58
Laplace, P S	46
Lewis, C.S.	59
Linear time	45-46
Logos	66
Meditation	48, 69-72, 95
Messiah	80
Michelangelo	38
Miller, Kenneth R.	27-28, 30, 32-35, 37
Mount Sinai	74
Muhammad	55-56, 69, 74, 79-82, 84-92, 111
Moral law	59, 96, 99-100, 109-110
Moral light	101
Moses	12, 19, 24, 56, 74-75, 81-82, 90, 92
Muslim	73, 84-85, 88, 91
Muslim law	85
Multiverse	37
Natural laws	35
Nirvana	70, 77
Noah	49, 74
Noble Eightfold Path	71
Non-random evolution	27
Nostradamus	48
Nuclear forces	95
Strong	94
Weak	94
Paleozoic era	20
Parmenides	66

Penca, Gerald F.	41
Physical constants	36
Pickthall, Mohammed M.	14
Pope John Paul II	106
Pope Pius XII	106
Pre-Cambrian	29
Proterozoic era	18
Protestants, Irish	55
Punctuated evolution	31, 42
Quantum mechanics	32
Quantum theory	32, 62
Qurān	13, 52, 69, 82-87, 89-91
Random mutation	28-30
Randomness	32, 94
Red Sea	74
Relativity	15, 21, 36, 45, 47, 62, 100
Relative time	22, 46, 48
Resurrection	58, 81-82, 89, 111
Sayings	84, 89
Schroeder, Gerald L.	18, 21, 28-29, 45-46, 49
Schwartz, Gary E.	37, 94-95
Selflessness	99, 101
Shemuel	39
Shiite	55-56
Source	11, 37, 70, 72, 91
Space-time	61-62
Sunnah	84, 87
Sunni	56
Supreme Being	11

Swarup, Ram	86, 88-89
Tabernacle	75, 90
Taoism	65, 69, 71-72
Ten Commandments	71, 109
Teleologist	97
Theory of General Relativity	15
Thermodynamics, second law	38
Traditions	84, 86, 88-89
Trinity	78-80
Torah	82, 84, 91
Tzu, Lao	65, 71
Universal consciousness	16, 20, 41, 48, 96, 100, 107, 109
Universal mind	95-96, 100
Upanishad, Brihad-aranyala	68
Upanishad, Maitri	68
Vedas	68
Virgin birth	58, 81
Wahy	86
Willy Wonka	103
Word	13, 81, 85-86, 92
Young earth creationists	27
Zeitgeist	96, 99-101

Bibliography

1. *The Holy Bible Containing the Old and New Testaments,* (Cleveland: World Publishing Company, 1611 edition).

2. R. Dawkins, *The God Delusion* (New York: Haughton Mifflin Co., 2006).

3. M.M. Pickthall, *The Meaning of the Glorious Quran* (London: The London Central Mosque Trust Limited, the Islamic Culture Center)

4. D. Filkin, *Stephen Hawking's Universe, The Cosmos Explained* (New York: HarperCollins, 1997).

5. S. Hawking, *A Brief History of Time* (New York: Bandam Press, 1996).

6. F. Capra, *The Tao of Physics* (Boulder: Shambhala Publications, 1975).

7. G. Brent Dalrymple, *The Age of the Earth* (Stanford: Stanford Press 1991).

8. G.L. Schroeder, *The Science of God* (New York: Broadway Books, 1997).

9. K.R. Miller, *Finding Darwin's God* (New York: HarperCollins, 1999).

10. Miller, ibid.

11. M. Tegmark, *Parallel Universes, in Science and Ultimate Reality: From Quantum to Cosmos* (Cambridge: Cambridge University Press, 2003)

12. G.E. Schwartz, *The G.O.D. Experiments* (New York: Atria Books, 2006).

13. http://www.edgarcayce.org/about_ec/cayce_ib/akashic/
    http://skepdic.com/akashic. .html
    http://en/wikipedia.org/wiki?Akashic_recilrs

14. R.L. Fox, *The Unauthorized Version* (London: Penguin, 1992).

15. A.N. Wilson, *Jesus* (Kibdib: Flamingo, 1993).

16. F. Collins, *The Language of God* (New York: Simon and Schuster, 2006).

17. L. Strobel, *The Case for Christ* (Grand Rapids: Zondervan, 1998).
18. G.R. Habermas, The Historical Jesus: Ancient Evidence for the Life of Christ (New York: College Press, 1996).
19. C.S. Lewis, *Mere Christianity* (Westwood: Barbour and Company, 1952).
20. S. Weinberg, *Dreams of a Final Theory* (London: Vintage, 1993).
21. J. Snelling, *The Buddhist Handbook, The Complete Guide to Buddhist Schools, Teaching, Practice, and History* (Rochester: Inner Traditions, 1991).
22. A. Jacobs, *The Essential Gostic Gospels, Including the Gospel of Thomas, The Gospel of Mary Magdalene* (London, Watkins Publishing, 2006).
23. R. Swarup. *Understanding the Hadith, the Sacred Traditions of Islam* (Amherst: Prometheus Books, 2002).
24. http://www.ebonmusings.org/atheism/new10c.html.